ADVANCED SCALES
and
DOUBLE STOPS
for
VIOLA

ISBN 978-0-7935-5629-8

G. SCHIRMER, Inc.

DISTRIBUTED BY

HAL•LEONARD®
CORPORATION
7777 W. BLUEMOUND RD. P.O. BOX 13819 MILWAUKEE, WI 53213

Advanced Scales and Double Stops for Viola

Leonard Mogill

C Major

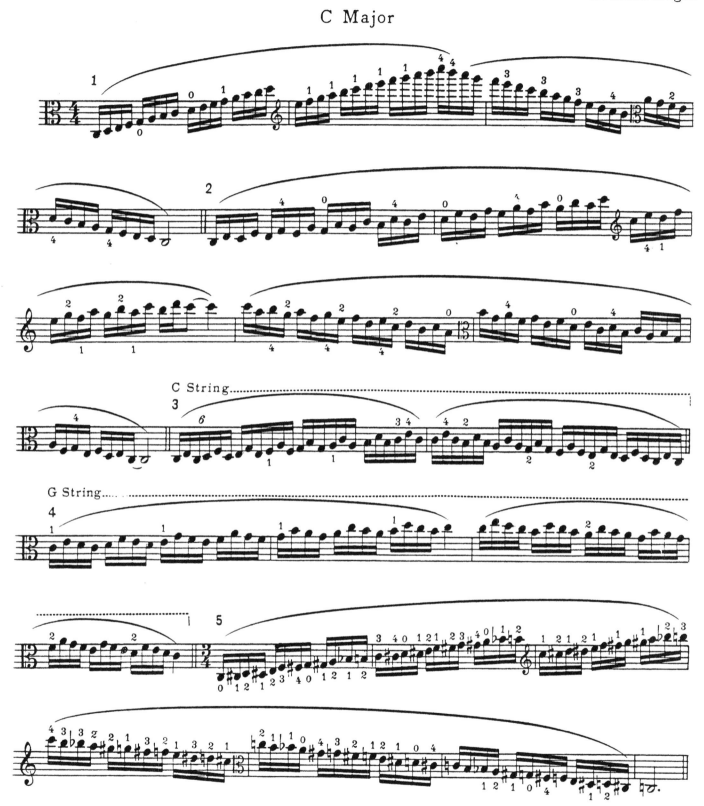

A Minor

A String

F Major

6

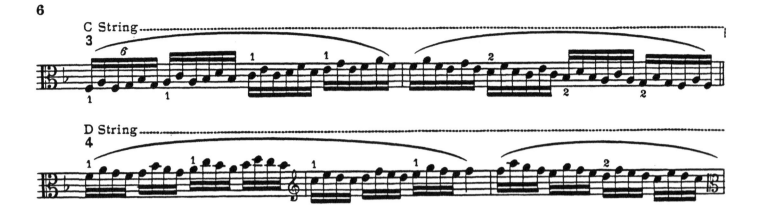

D Minor

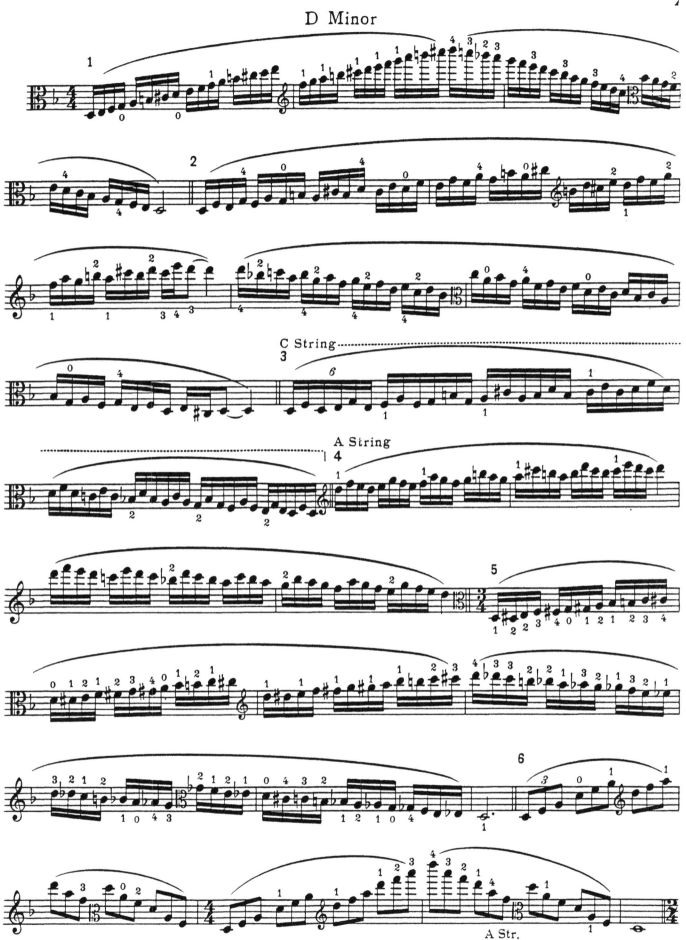

Bb Major

G Minor

G String

D String

Eb Major

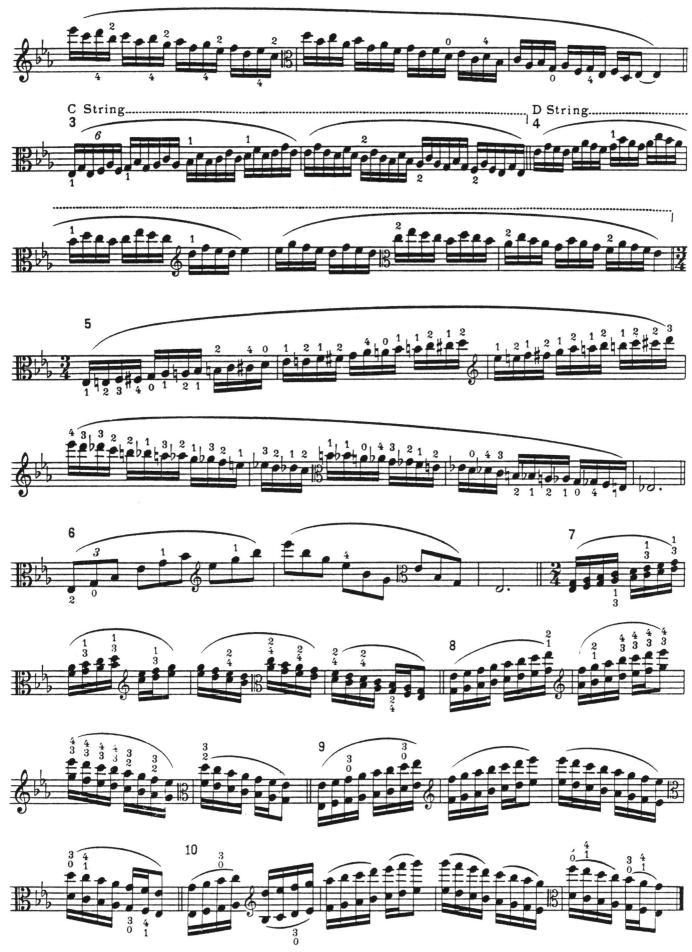

C Minor

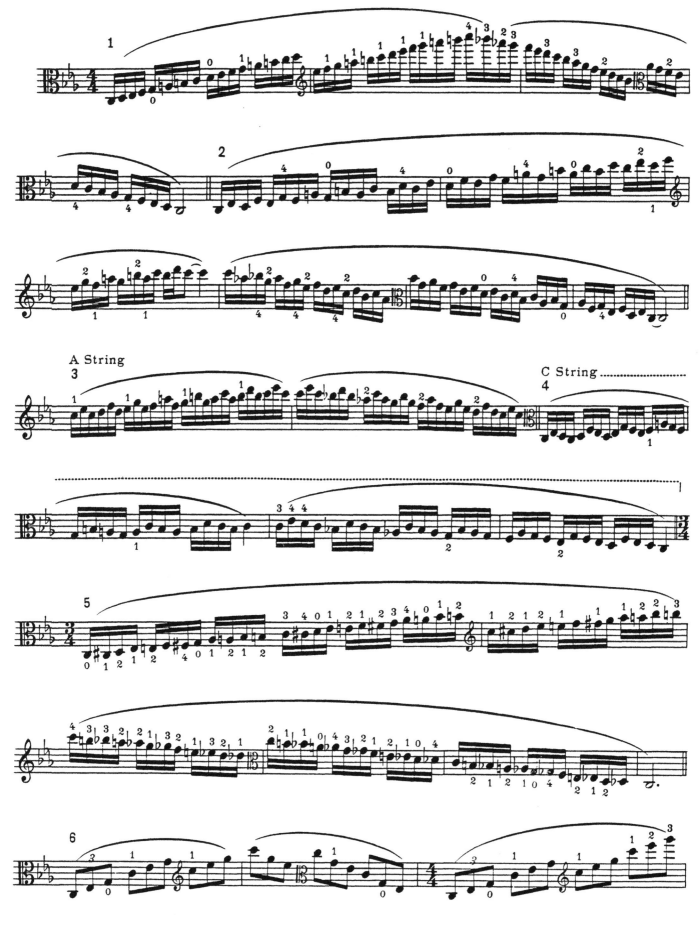

A Str.

9

10

Ab Major

1

2

G String

3

D String

4

F Minor

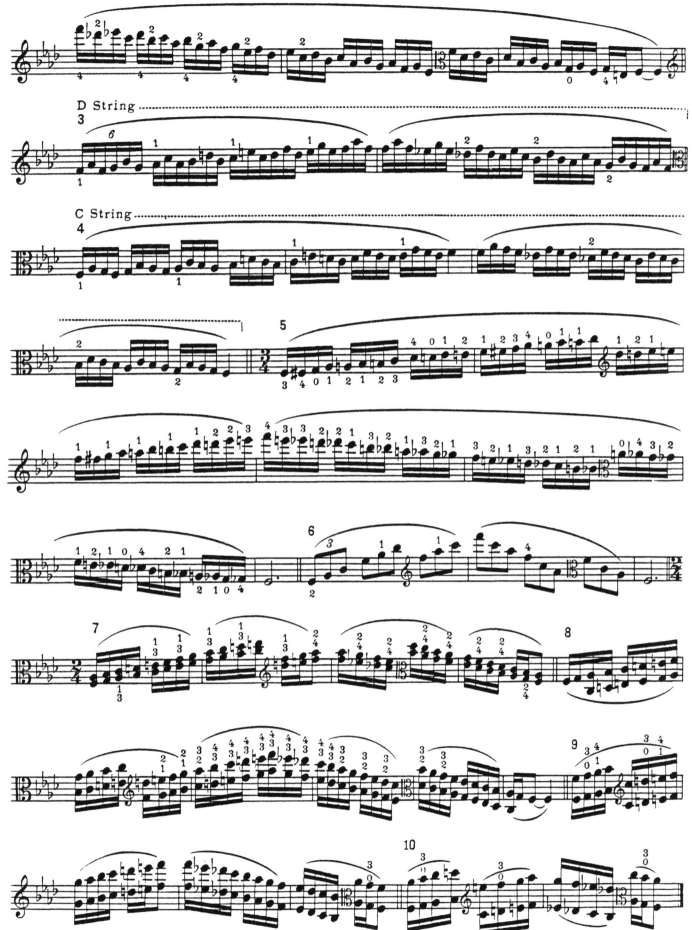

Db Major

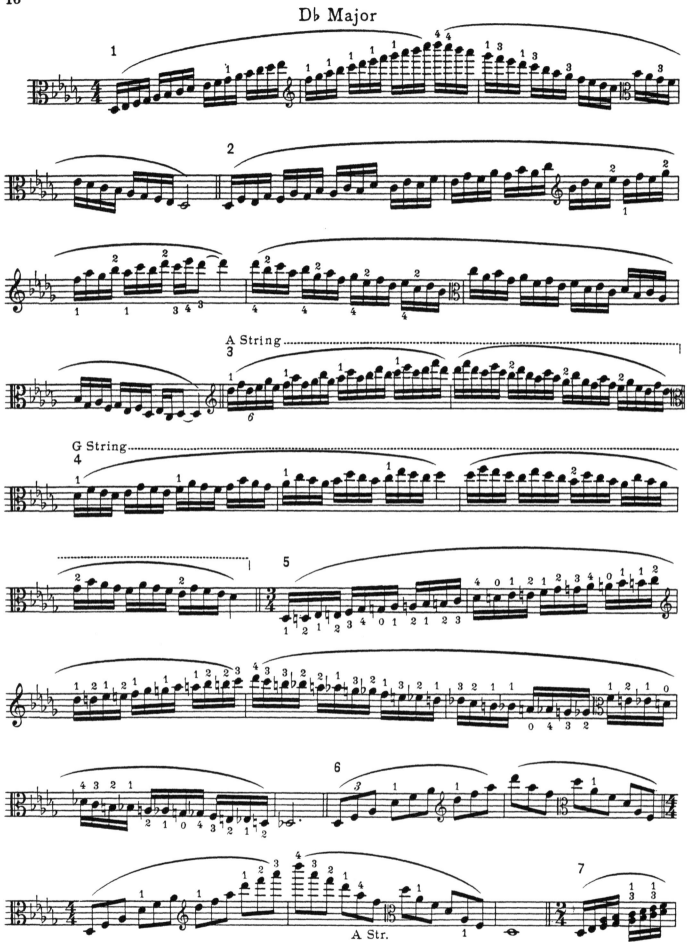

Bb Minor

Gb Major

Eb Minor

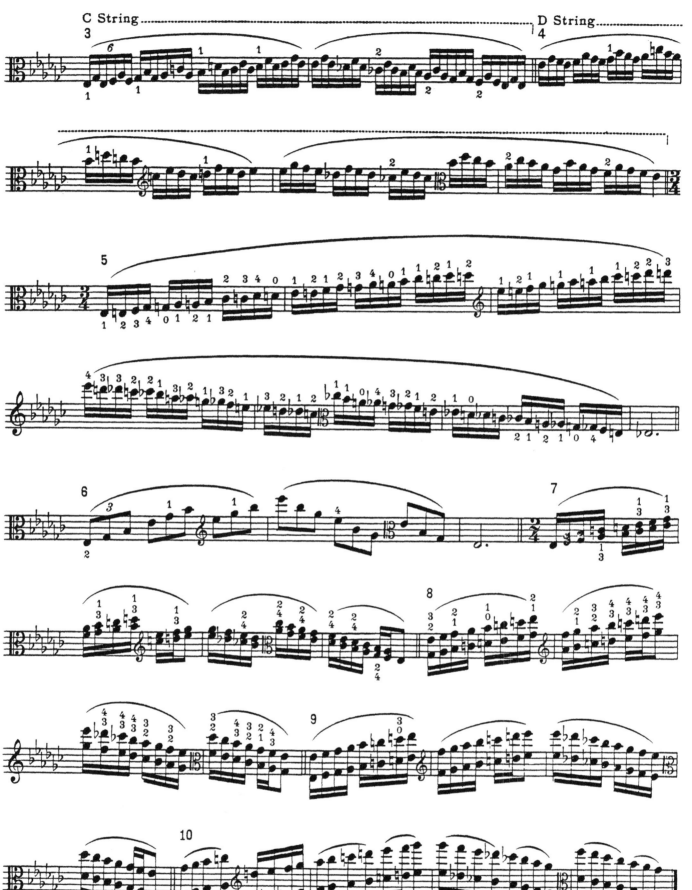

B Major

22

G# Minor

E Major

D String .... C String ....

C# Minor

A String

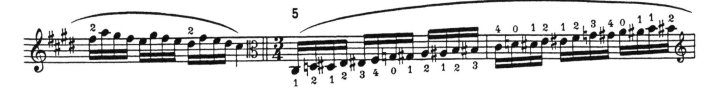

26

A Major

F♯ Minor

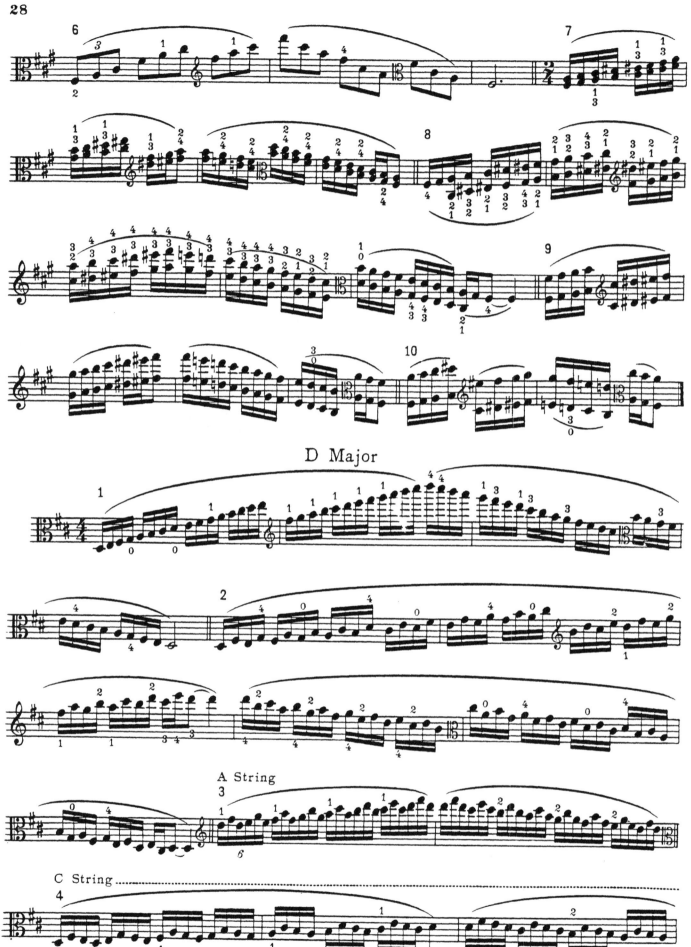

D Major

A String

C String

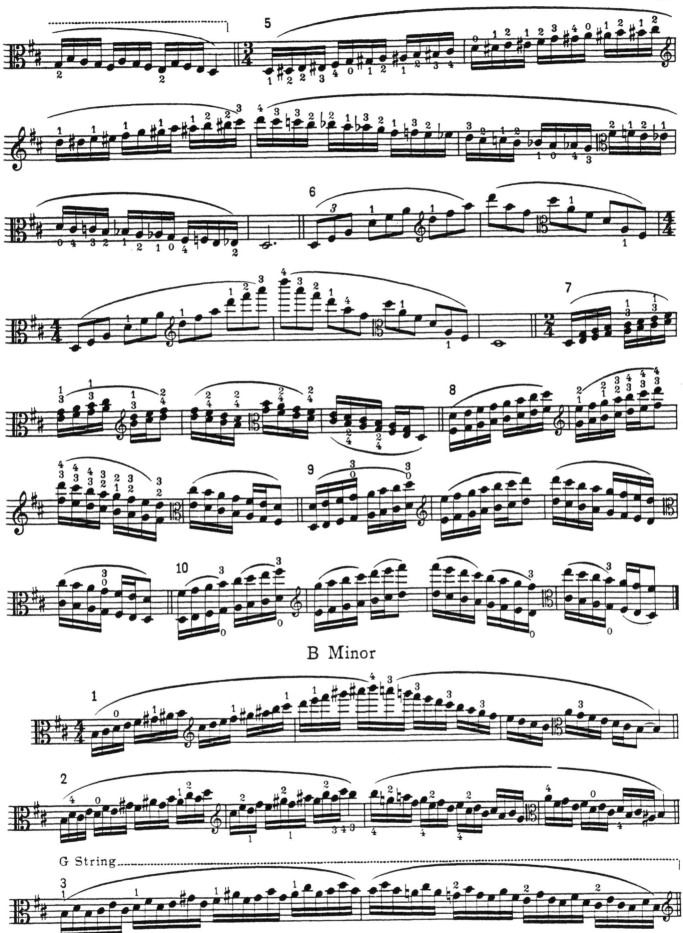

B Minor

A String

G Major

E Minor